Bug Butts

Bug Butts

By Dawn Cusick

Illustrations by Hande Levesque

EarlyLight Books

Waynesville, North Carolina, USA

Cataloging Information

Cusick, Dawn.
    Bug butts/ written by Dawn Cusick; illustrated by Haude Levesque.
        48 p. : col. ill. ; 20 cm.
    Summary: Explores the range of behavior used by a variety of insects,
        including beetles that spray acid from anal glands, caterpillars
        that shoot frass from their anal glands, spittle bugs that blow
        bubbles with their anal glands, and 20 more examples.
    LC: QL 494
    Dewey: 595.7
    ISBN-13: 978-0-9797455-0-8 (alk. paper)
    ISBN-10: 0-9797455-0-0 (alk. paper)
        Insects – Juvenile literature
        Insects – Anatomy – Juvenile literature

Text & Cover Design: Thom Gaines
Technical Editor: Dr. Timothy Forrest
Page Layout: Beth Fielding
Copy Editor: Susan Brill

10 9 8 7 6 5 4 3 2 1

First edition

Published by EarlyLight Books, Inc.
1436 Dellwood Road
Waynesville, NC 28786

Distributed by BookMasters, Inc.

Manufactured in China.

ISBN-13: 978-0-9797455-0-8
ISBN-10: 0-9797455-0-0

To Aymeric, for his
encouragement and support

—HL

To my favorite entomologists
— Tim, Jen, and Jim —
with respect and affection

—DC

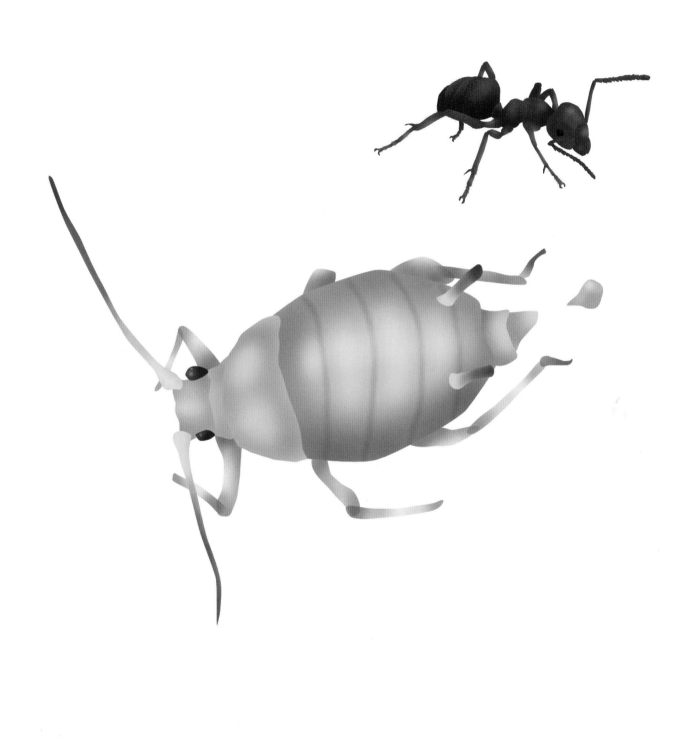

Bug Butts

Contents

CHAPTER 1

Bug

Bubble Butts

Remember how much fun it was to blow bubbles when you were little? Suppose you could blow bubbles from your butt? Pretty cool, huh?

Spittlebugs eat lots of sugary plant sap when they're young nymphs, so they excrete lots of fluid through their butts. When the fluid comes out of their butts, they move their abdomens (the area near their stomachs) up and down to make bubbles. They keep making bubbles until their entire bodies are covered with bubbles.

The bubbles keep their young bodies from getting too hot or too cold, plus help them hide from predators. After the spittlebugs go through their final molt, they climb out of the bubbles and live the rest of their lives as bubble-free adults.

Breathing Butts

Dragonfly nymphs live underwater and are ferocious hunters, eating mosquito larvae, tadpoles, crayfish, and anything else they can catch. To breathe underwater, the dragonflies have gills in the rectal chambers inside their butts. The water flows into their anal openings when dragonflies open their anal valves. Oxygen in the water moves across the gills and into tubes called trachea.

Many other types of insects spend lots of time underwater, hiding from predators. To get air underwater, they have long siphons—sort of like a snorkel—that come out of their buts and up to the water's surface. You can call these bugs Snorkel Butts!

Wait, there's more! Dragonfly nymphs can also use their breathing system for quick escapes and movement. When they hunt on the surface of the water, they can squirt water from their butts so fast that it shoots them forward. This type of movement is called fluid propulsion and is similar to the way jet skis move forward through water at fast speeds.

Spraying Butts

Many species of ants have a great way to make predators leave them alone — they spray them with acid! The acid is stored in a space right behind their butts. When ants are disturbed by predators, the ants squeeze the muscles around their anal openings and the acid sprays out. The acid stings the predator and makes the ants taste bad if predators eat them.

Some species of cockroaches, dobsonflies, caterpillars, and beetles also spray enemies with acid from their butts. This type of protection is called chemical defense.

Wait, there's more! Some types of ground crickets squirt a stinky, glue-like substance out of their butts when a predator tries to attack them. The substance is so sticky that the predator's legs get stuck together!

Exploding Butts

African bombardier beetles definitely get the prize for best chemical butt defense. These beetles have two separate compartments inside their butts, one to store acid and another to store special enzymes. When the beetles need to fight off an enemy, they mix the chemicals in both compartments together, which causes a small explosion. The explosion pushes acid out of the beetles' butts with a lot of force, so predators get hit in the face with hot, stinky acid.

Scientists have done experiments that show the beetles can aim the acid wherever they want, which lets them fight off ants or other enemies that might attack them from any direction. Scientists still don't know how the beetles keep the acid from damaging their own exoskeletons.

Spinning Butts

Have you ever seen a spider web and wondered where the silk came from? Most spiders spin silk with spinerettes at the back ends of their bodies — their butts!

Beetles also spin silk from their butts. When young beetles (called weevils) need to make cocoons, they raise their butts high in the air and spin a silk cocoon onto a leaf. The weevils stay in their cocoons for about a week while their bodies finish developing, then they push their way out of the cocoons with their adult bodies.

Wait, there's more! Antlion and lacewing larvae also spin silk from their butts. When it's time to pupate, they dig small holes in the ground and cover themselves with silk in underground cocoons.

Shooting Butts

Skipper caterpillars have a special part of their body, the anal comb, that lets them shoot their frass pellets (their poop!) far away from their bodies. They use a combination of pressure in their abdomens and muscles in their anal prolegs to launch the frass pellets.

Why would skipper caterpillars shoot their poop? Are they playing games? Trying to hit birds? Or practicing 3-point basketball shots? Nope.

When they're not eating, skipper caterpillars spend most of their time hiding from predators and keeping their bodies cool in rolled-up leaves. Scientists have done experiments that show that preadatory wasps, who like to eat caterpillars, use the caterpillars' poop to find the caterpillars in their leaves. Caterpillars that shoot their poop far away are less likely to be found — and eaten! — by the wasps.

Take a Guess: How far can caterpillars shoot their poop? Up to 40 times farther than the length of their bodies!

Building Butts

Some caterpillars have a big problem. They need to eat a lot of leaves while they're growing, but sometimes their favorite leaves are on plants defended by ants. The ants attack the caterpillars on their plants — biting and killing them.

To solve this problem, some caterpillars make special hiding places called frass chains on the edges of leaves. The chains are made from poop pellets that are tied together with silk, and work sort of like a hanging ladder. The ants dislike the frass chains and don't attack the caterpillars on them. Some plants have so many ants on them that the caterpillars spend all of their time — except when they're eating — sitting on or hanging from their frass chains.

Wait, there's more! Ever wonder why the ants don't want caterpillars on their leaves? Because they're taking care of insects that poop honeydew, which the ants like to eat! (See pages 36 and 43 for more about honeydew-pooping bugs.)

Umbrella Butts

On a rainy day, you may protect yourself from the rain by holding an umbrella over your head. If you're a small, defenseless, tortoise beetle, you need to protect yourself from something much worse than rain. Hungry birds, frogs, and bigger bugs spend their days searching for you, hungry for an afternoon snack. What to do? Build an umbrella to hide under, of course!

Larval tortoise beetles have long spines on the backs of their bodies called anal forks. The beetles' poop moves out of their anuses and onto their anal forks, where it creates an umbrella shape called a fecal shield. Sometimes the beetles mix their old molted skin in with the poop. The fecal shield looks like an umbrella, and protects the beetles by hiding them from predators and keeping parasites away.

Wait, there's more! Another species of tortoise beetle has a different way to hide from predators and fight off parasites. Their poop comes out in long, skinny strands that looks like hair. The beetles cover their bodies in the hair-like poop and live under it until they're adults!

CHAPTER 2

Run for Your Life!

How would you warn your friends or family about big trouble if you couldn't use words? Flower thrips can't send their family and friends a text message or jump up and down, waving their arms, to warn them when a predator appears. Instead, they squeeze a drop of liquid from their butts onto a flower or leaf. Chemicals in this anal liquid send a message to nearby thrips to run and hide — quick! quick! — before they are eaten by a hungry predator.

Wait, there's more! Female fruit flies have glands in their anal cavities (their butts!) that produce chemicals called pheromones. The pheromones send messages to males, kind of like yelling, "Hello, I'm looking for a boyfriend!" Male fruit flies are very good at recognizing this message and come running (or flying, in this case) as fast as they can.

Follow the Leader

Weevils (shown here) and caterpillars face the same challenge every day. They need to eat a lot of food, but leaving their homes alone to find tasty leaves can be dangerous. Birds, frogs, lizards, and other insects all want to eat them! To protect themselves, some weevils and caterpillars leave their homes in large groups, following each other, single file, through forests to their feeding sites.

When you watch caterpillars moving in a line (called a "procession"), it looks like each caterpillar has stuck its face to the butt of the caterpillar ahead of it. Actually, the caterpillars are following a special chemical trail (made from pheromones) that each caterpillar puts down through an opening on the underside of its body.

Think Quick: Why are weevils and caterpillars so hungry? Because they need to store energy to use while they are transforming into beetles, butterflies, and moths in their cocoons.

Wait, there's more! After they eat, some types of weevils and caterpillars rest together in a circular shape with their butts facing the inside of the circle and their heads facing out.

Home, Sweet Home

Suppose you went away on a long trip. On your way back, you realized that someone had taken away every road sign, street name, and house number. How would you find your way back home?

Cockroaches often have to travel far from home to find food. To return home, cockroaches use special chemicals in their poop (called pheromones) to mark their trail. Every time they find another piece of their frass, they know they are going in the right direction.

More Butt Talk: Bark beetles also use their poop to communicate. As the beetles eat their way through a tree's bark, they leave poop trails with their pheromones in it. The more beetles that poop in the tree, the stronger the pheromones and the easier it is for even more beetles to find the tree.

CHAPTER 3

Tasty

Treats!

Bug Butt Buffet

Some aphids, thorn bugs, treehoppers, and froghoppers have a special relationship — called mutualism — with ants. These bugs suck lots of sap from plants so their excrement (a sort of liquid poop) is great food for ants. The liquid poop is called honeydew, and is full of sugar, protein, and vitamins. The ants live on the same plants as the aphids and hoppers and get an all-they-can-eat poop buffet. In return, the ants protect the hoppers and thorn bugs from predators. Pretty cool, huh?

Sometimes the ants eat the honeydew off the leaves where aphids and other insects leave it. Other times the ants drink directly from the aphid's anus. In some species, ants let the aphids or hoppers know that they want a drink by tapping on the bug's abdomen with their antennae. When the aphid or hopper feels an ant's antennae tap, it lifts its butt so the ant can drink.

Butt Juice to the Rescue!

Some species of cockroaches and termites eat wood as part of their regular diet. Unfortunately, their intestines can't break down the cellulose in the wood. What's a hungry termite or cockroach to do? Termites have lots of small animals (microorganisms called *Trichonympha*) that live in their intestines to digest the cellulose for them!

Newborn cockroaches and termites aren't born with *Trichonympha* in their intestines, so they drink liquid from a family member's butt to get the microorganisms into their intestines. Every time young cockroaches and termites go through a growth spurt (a molt), they lose their microorganisms again and have to drink more butt juice.

Have your parents ever paid you a few bucks for washing the car or doing yard work? Well thank your lucky stars you're not a termite! A termite queen lets her workers drink a high-energy juice from her butt for building and guarding her nest.

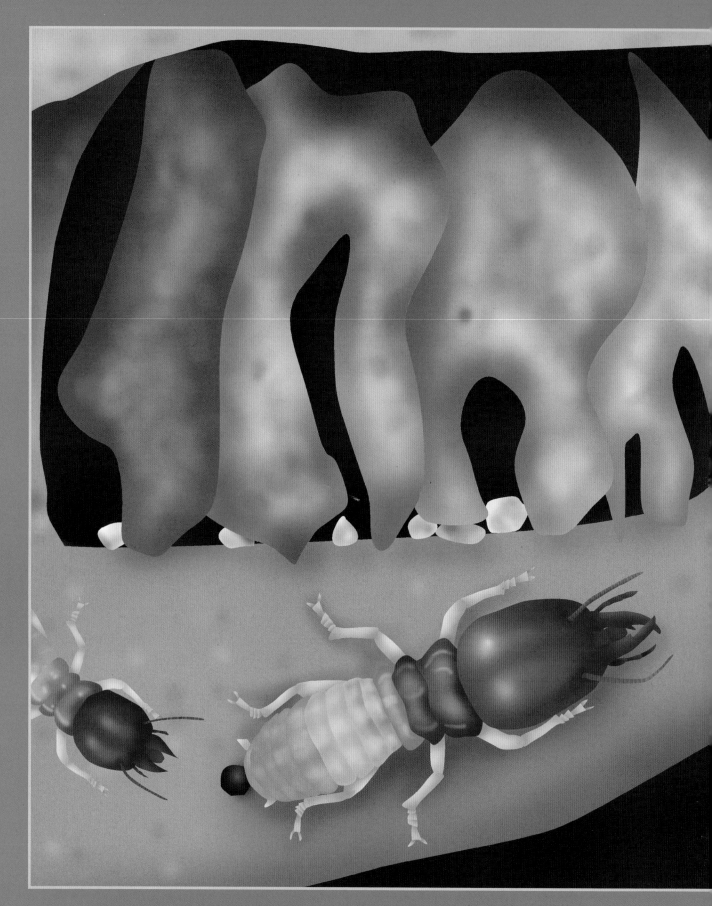

Poop Farmers

While some bugs work hard to get rid of their feces, some termites keep their poop and use it in some really cool ways. Termites arrange their fecal pellets into piles in their underground nests, then they use the feces like well-fertilized soil to grow their favorite food — fungus! Some species of ants and beetles also grow fungi on fecal pellets.

Wait, there's more! Termites in Australia and Africa mix their poop with spit and sand and use the mixture to build houses (called termitaria) for large colonies. Some of the houses they build are taller than four cars stacked on top of each other!

Better than a Spoon!

The sugary honeydew secreted from the butts of some aphids, treehoppers, froghoppers, and thorn bug nymphs can cause a big problem. Mold grows very quickly wherever honeydew lands. And, since mold can kill a nymph if it grows on its body, nymphs have to be extra-careful of where they poop.

Some hoppers and thorn bugs don't have to worry about honeydew mold because the ants that protect them eat the honeydew directly from their butts. Other hoppers and thorn bugs give honeydew to ants in a different way. They have a short anal whip that sticks out from the back of their bodies.

For a while, some scientists thought that hoppers and thorn bugs were using their anal whips to fight off predators. When they did some experiments, they found out this wasn't true. Instead, the bugs use their anal whips to place drops of honeydew in a half-circle shape around them for the ants to eat. Hoppers and thorn bugs that don't live with caretaking ants have much longer anal whips. The longer whips allow them to place the honeydew farther from their bodies.

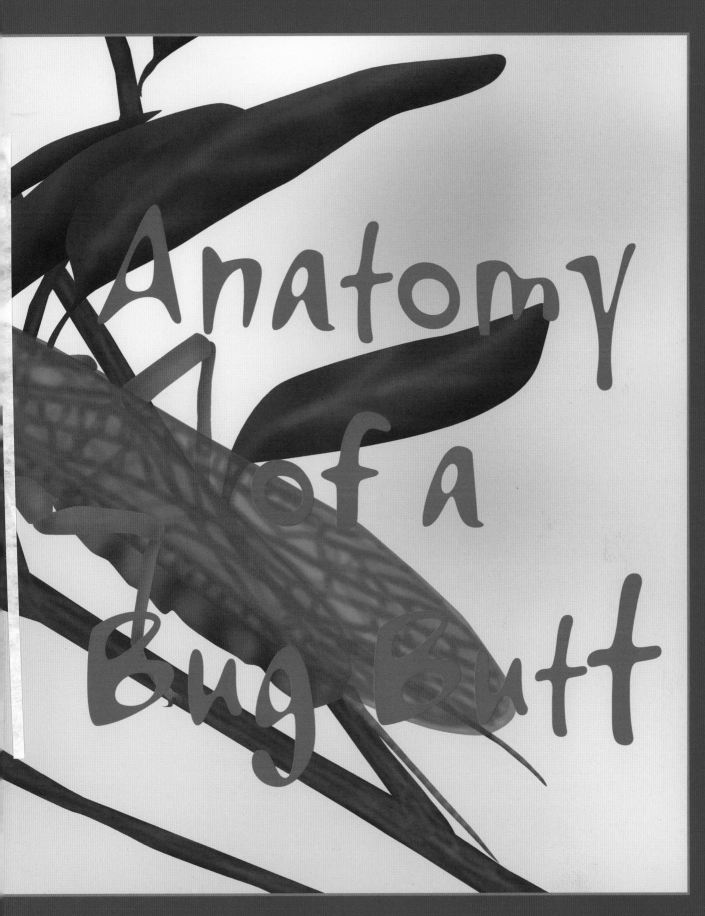

Anatomy
of a
Bug Butt

Bug Butt Butts

What, exactly, is a bug butt? In some ways, a bug's butt is a lot like yours. Both insects (the scientific word for bugs) and humans have an alimentary canal. The alimentary canal starts with the mouth and ends with the anus. (The word anus is another word for butt.) The alimentary canal is a long, tube in animals where food is brought into the body and digested. Leftover waste leaves the body from the anus. Biologists call the leftover waste in an insect frass or feces. Most kids call the leftover waste poop.

If you look closely at an insect, you can see the mouth at the front end of the body and the anus at the back end. You cannot see the rest of the alimentary canal because it is deep inside the insect's body, protected by layers of muscle and tissue and a hard exoskeleton on the outside. The picture below shows the three main sections of an insect's body: the head, the thorax, and the abdomen. Some insects also have one or two pairs of wings.

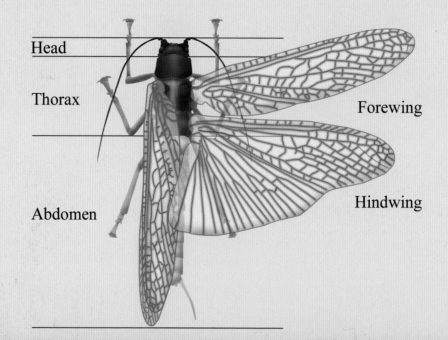

Head

Thorax

Forewing

Hindwing

Abdomen

If you were to look inside an insect's body, the alimentary canal would look like the picture below. There are three main areas: the foregut, near the mouth; the midgut in the middle; and the hindgut in the back.

Food comes into a bug's foregut from its mouth. Sometimes the food stays in the foregut awhile before moving to the midgut. In the midgut, food is broken down into small pieces (molecules). The molecules move into the hemolymph, a fluid that works in insects the way blood works in people. Good food molecules are used by the insect's body to build muscles and other important tasks. Bad molecules are absorbed by the Malpighian tubules and moved into the hindgut, where they become part of the insect's poop (or feces or frass). Poop in the hindgut gets pushed out of the insect's body through its anus, or butt.

As the insects in this book show, bugs use their butts for lots of things besides pooping. These adaptations help them escape from predators, get food, communicate with family members, and much more. The only thing more amazing than the bugs you have read about here are the bugs you will find on your own outdoor adventures!

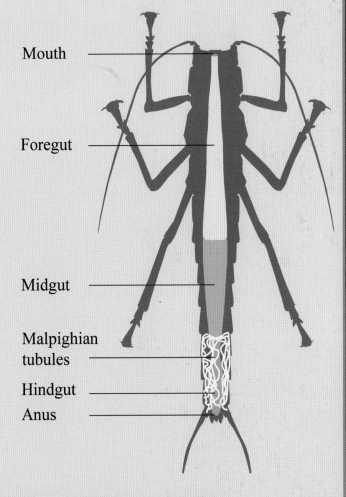

Mouth

Foregut

Midgut

Malpighian tubules

Hindgut

Anus

Index

Glossary

Larvae are very young insects. When they are small, they do not look anything like adults. Larvae make cocoons around themselves to finish developing into their adult shapes.

When **larvae** enter their cocoons, they **pupate.** While they are in their cocoons, they are called **pupae,** not larvae. Insects such as butterflies and moths develop as **larvae** and **pupae.**

Nymphs are also young insects, but when they hatch from their eggs, they look like very small adults. Insects such as crickets and katydids develop as **nymphs.**

When **nymphs** outgrow their exoskeletons (the hard, outer layers of their bodies), they **molt.** To **molt,** an insect climbs out of its old, outer skin. Some **nymphs molt** many times before they become adults.

Acknowledgments

Biologists who study insects are called entomologists. Some entomologists are teachers, some are writers, some are researchers, and some do all three. The research, writing, and teaching of the following entomologists provided much of the factual information for this book: Dr. W.J. Baumgartne, Dr. Paulien J.A de Brujin, Dr. Stanley Caveney, Dr. James Costa, Dr. Leon Dufour, Dr. Martijn Egas, Dr. Maria Eisner, Dr. Thomas Eisner, Dr. Timothy Forrest, Dr. Arne Janssen, Dr. Heather McLean, Dr. Maurice Sabelis, and Dr. David Surry, and Dr. Martha Weiss.

The illustrator would like to thank the following people who generously provided technical assistance:
Dr. Ralph Holzenthal, for lending specimens and critiquing illustrations;
Dr. Thomas Eisner, for photo use and technical feedback on the African bombardier beetle illustration;
Dr. Paulo Oliveira, for photo use and technical feedback on the frass-chain caterpillar illustration;
Dr. Martha Weiss for information about the silverspotted caterpillar and technical feedback on the illustration;
Dr. Terrence Fitzgerald for sharing tent caterpillar photographs; Dr. Ayako Wada Kadsumata for sharing cockroach photographs;
Dr. Aanen Duur, for sharing termite information, photographs, and providing technical feedback on the illustration;
and Dr. Mark Asplen, for sharing information about aphid behavior.